ENDGAME

FINDING GOD AMONG EARTH'S MIGHTIEST HEROES

SCOTT BAYLES

CONTENTS

INTRODUCTION

If you've read any of my books or met me in person, you already know that I'm a super-geek. I've been collecting comic-books since I was a kid, our family cosplays at comic-conventions, and I get super excited every time there's a new superhero movie in theaters.

However, for more than a decade now, Marvel Studios has proven that superheroes aren't just for comic-book nerds like myself. Marvel has taken their beloved comic-book characters and adapted them into a string of box-office blockbusters. Unlike other movie studios that create standalone movies or sequels, Marvel created an entire universe of interconnected characters and stories, spanning more than twenty movies that crescendoed in 2019's release of *Avengers: Endgame*. As the culmination of twenty-plus movies, *Endgame* made a massive cultural impact and broke all sorts of records on its march to become the highest grossing movie of all time. *Avengers: Endgame* grossed $2.8 billion in the box-office, making it one of the most watched and most influential films in popular culture. For that reason, I think Marvel's box-office bombshell is worth examining through the lens of faith.

I absolutely love finding spiritual meaning in superhero movies and sharing Christ through comics. So, I'd like to invite you to join me as I deconstruct some of the characters and story arcs from *Avengers: Endgame* to see what they might be able to teach us about faith, life, and God.

Chapter One: Hawkeye

The opening scene of *Avengers: Endgame* focuses on Clint Barton, better known as Hawkeye. In the previous film, *Avenger: Infinity War*, Iron Man, Thor, Captain America and the rest of the Avengers unite to battle their most powerful enemy yet—the Mad Titan, Thanos. On a mission to collect six gems of incredible power (known as the Infinity Stones), Thanos plans to use the ancient artifacts to wipe out half of all life in the universe. Although the Avengers valiantly oppose him, they fail. And, with the snap of his fingers, billions of lives turned to ash, carried aloft by the wind.

Thanos won.

Hawkeye, however, stayed out of the fray in *Infinity War*. He resigned from the Avengers and walked away from the superhero life to spend more time with his family. Unfortunately, even though he avoided the battle, Hawkeye still experienced a devastating loss when Thanos snapped his fingers.

In the opening scene of *Endgame*, we see Hawkeye, Clint Barton, enjoying a picnic with his wife and three children. Clint smiles and laughs while teaching his daughter to utilize a bow and arrow. His two boys play catch with an old baseball and worn-out gloves. His wife, Laura, sets the picnic table and asks everyone what they want on their hot dogs. The scene is filled with charm and cheerfulness. But, suddenly, everything changes.

Laura calls the family to the table and Clint turns to his daughter, but she's not there. Ashes float through the air where she once stood. Confused, Clint looks around, then turns back toward Laura and the boys. But they've vanished, as well. Panic spreads across Clint's face as his eyes dart in every direction, searching for his family. He calls out their names. But no reply comes. Nothing is left of them but dust blown by the wind.

In a moment, in the blink of an eye, Hawkeye lost his whole family—all the people he loved most in the world. Can you imagine what that would be like? How do you deal with a tragedy of that magnitude? Hawkeye doesn't deal with it very well.

His grief drives him to some dark places. It doesn't seem fair to him that innocent people like his wife and children disappeared while lowlifes and evildoers still walk the streets. So, he goes rogue and begins taking out his anger and anguish by hunting down and killing crooks and criminals all across the globe. Hawkeye allows himself to be swallowed up by his misery and mourning.

If there's one Biblical figure who could relate to Hawkeye's story, it's Job. Many of you are probably familiar with Job's tragic tale. His story is told in the book that bears his name. The Bible says that Job was a good man, who loved God and stayed away from evil. One day, an unexpected messenger arrived at Job's door with news: "Enemies have raided your fields. They stole all your oxen and killed all the farmhands!" While that messenger was still speaking, another out-of-breath messenger arrived: "There's been a fire! All of your sheep and shepherds are dead!" Then another messenger arrived, "A band of raiders has stolen your camels and killed your servants!" Finally, one last messenger arrived with the worst news of all: "Your sons and daughters were eating together at your son's house when a powerful wind swept in and demolished the house. All of your children are dead."

In a moment, in an instant, Job lost everything—his herds, his flocks, his livelihood, and most importantly his children. The people he loved most in this world—gone, just like that. Like, Hawkeye, Job was overwhelmed with grief. When he heard the news, the Bible says, "Job stood up and tore his robe in grief" (Job 1:20 NLT). The ripping of one's robe was an ancient custom that symbolized the rending of one's heart.

I pray none of you ever experience loss on this level, but we all experience trauma and tragedy. Your house burns down. You get laid off. The doctor calls with the worst possible news. The divorce papers arrive. A loved one passes away. Traumatic events are all too common. So, the question is—how do you respond when trouble or tragedy finds you? How do you live through a bad day, a bad week, a bad month, or even a bad year?

Like Hawkeye, we can allow our heartache to consume us and lead us down a dark path, but I think that Job shows us a better way. Job survived this calamity with his faith intact— which is pretty impressive, all things considered. Job's example reveals three things we all need in order to deal effectively with heartache and hardship. The first thing we need to cope with calamity is faith.

FAITH

Job was a man of faith both before and after disaster struck. Just look at what Job does immediately after tearing his robe in grief. The Bible says: Then he shaved his head and fell to the ground to worship. He said, "I came naked from my mother's womb, and I will be naked when I leave. The Lord gave me what I had, and the Lord has taken it away. Praise the name of the Lord!" (Job 1:20-21 NLT).

Despite his suffering, Job trusted God's will for his life and continued to praise him. This is a remarkable testament to Job's faith. Rather than allowing this tragedy to destroy his faith and his relationship with God, Job worships God. He draws closer to God.

Through faith, Job knows that God is there with him in the midst of his suffering. His faith gives him solace and the strength to overcome his sorrow. Faith can see us through the storms of life. Honestly, I don't know how people cope with life's sorrows and suffering if they don't have faith in God.

Job's faith wasn't naive, either. Later, Job asks his wife, "Should we accept only good things from the hand of God and never anything bad?" (Job 2:10 NLT). Many people have the mistaken belief that because they're Christians or because they go to church every Sunday that God is somehow obligated to shelter and protect them from tragedies or traumas—that nothing really bad should ever happen to them. But Job understood that bad things don't just happen to bad people. Bad things happen to good people all the time. Jesus put it this way: "He causes his sun to rise on the evil and the good, and sends rain on the righteous and the unrighteous" (Matthew 5:45 NIV).

Unlike nonbelievers, however, Christians know that God can use our trials and tribulations to bring about something good in our lives. In fact, that's a promise. Scripture assures us, "We know that all things work together for the good of those who love God; those who are called according to His purpose" (Romans 8:28 HCSB).

I know there have been countless times when this verse has rung true in my life, and I'm sure there have been in yours, too. Let's face it—bad things happen and they happen with unpredictable frequency and varying levels of intensity. Some are mere inconveniences; others are life-shattering disasters. But this promise can meet every heartache or hardship head-on. It's an iron-clad, unfailing, all-encompassing, God-given guarantee that every single circumstance of life will sooner or later turn out well for those who love God.

So, when your world feels like it's falling apart, cling to this promise. Trust in God. Have faith. Job first demonstrates that coping with catastrophe requires faith. Furthermore, to effectively deal with disaster, we need friends.

FRIENDS

This is something Hawkeye and Job have in common. In the movie, Hawkeye's closest friend is Natasha, better known as Black Widow. When Hawkeye goes off the grid, Natasha starts searching for him. Years go by, but she doesn't give up. Finally, she tracks him to Tokyo where she finds him battling some Yakuza (Japanese mafia), and confronts him. "You shouldn't be here," Hawkeye tells her. But Black Widow replies, "Neither should you... killing all these people isn't going to bring your family back." She then takes Clint by the hand and encourages him to rejoin the team, where he'd be surrounded by friends. She gives him hope that together they might be able to put things right.

Similarly, shortly after the death of his family, Job's friends visited him. The Bible says, "When three of Job's friends heard of the tragedy he had suffered, they got together and traveled from their homes to comfort and console him" (Job 2:11 NLT).

One of the reasons that God created the church is so that we'd have friends and family to comfort and console us when tragedy comes our way. The Bible says, "Praise be to the God… of all comfort, who comforts us in all our troubles, so that we can comfort those in any trouble with the comfort we ourselves receive from God" (2 Corinthians 1:3-4 NIV).

Unfortunately, all too often people withdraw from their friends and family when life gets tough. Maybe they're going through a divorce, or wrestling with depression, or dealing with some other disaster and they feel like they just can't face their friends or family. So, they stop socializing. They stop going to church.

If you're dealing with some tragedy in your life, you need to know that it's easier when you have the loving support of your church family. But the rest of us need to follow Black Widow's example. She sought out her hurting friend. She went to him. Job's friends did the same thing. They didn't wait for Job to come to them for help. They traveled to him.

Some of you may be thinking, "I just don't know what to do in those situations. I don't know what to say to make someone feel better." You don't have to say anything. Look at what Job's friends did: "When they saw Job from a distance, they scarcely recognized him. Wailing loudly, they tore their robes and threw dust into the air over their heads to show their grief. Then they sat on the ground with him for seven days and nights. No one said a word to Job, for they saw that his suffering was too great for words" (Job 2:12-13 NLT). These are good friends. We all need friends like these. They grieved with him, they shared his sorrow, and then they just sat there silently supporting him for a week.

Of course, when that week was over, they got into some pretty heated discussions. For the next 35 chapters, they question Job and argue with him about the nature of sin and evil, the justice and goodness of God, and the human condition.

Honestly, things seem to go downhill as soon as they open their mouths. Sometimes, the best thing you can do for someone handling hardship is to just be there. Don't say a word. Just show up.

In order to survive life-shattering disasters, we need faith, we need friends, and, finally, we need foresight.

FORESIGHT

Job was able to cope with his tragedy because he had foresight. He could look beyond the here and now. Specifically, Job looked forward to the day of resurrection.

During an impassioned reply to one of his friends, Job announces, "But as for me, I know that my Redeemer lives, and he will stand upon the earth at last. And after my body has decayed, yet in my body I will see God! I will see him for myself. Yes, I will see him with my own eyes. I am overwhelmed at the thought!" (Job 19:25-27 NLT).

Despite his brokenness and bereavement, Job remained completely confident that death is not the end. The grave is not the final word. Job knew God's endgame. He knew that someday, in the distant future, God would raise him from the dead and he would see God face to face. He could endure the hardships and heartaches of here and now because he could look forward with hope to the hereafter.

One of the reasons Hawkeye couldn't cope with his loss is that he didn't have any hope of ever seeing his family again. When Black Widow tells him that the Avengers have come with a plan to bring everyone back, he tells her, "Don't do that... Don't give me hope." She replied, "I wish I could have given it to you sooner."

As Christians, we have hope! We know that we will see many of our loved ones again. Paul addresses that very issue. He writes:

"And now, dear brothers and sisters, we want you to know what will happen to the believers who have died so you will not grieve like people who have no hope. For since we believe that Jesus died and was raised to life again, we also believe that when Jesus returns, God will bring back with him the believers who have died... For the Lord himself will come down from heaven with a commanding shout, with the voice of the archangel, and with the trumpet call of God. First, the believers who have died will rise from their graves. Then, together with them, we who are still alive and remain on the earth will be caught up in the clouds to meet the Lord in the air. Then we will be with the Lord forever. So encourage each other with these words." (1 Thessalonians 4:13-18 NLT)

This is the hope that we have in Christ. The day of Christ's return will be a day of resurrections, reunions, and rejoicing. You and I can look forward to a future free from hardships and heartaches. God promises that he will wipe every tear from our eyes. There will be no more death or disasters, no more suffering or sorrow, no more crying or calamities, no more pain or problems. All these things will be gone forever. Knowing what God has in store for us in the future ought to make our burdens and broken hearts much easier to bear in the present.

***

Remarkably, both Job and Hawkeye have happy endings. In the movie, the Avengers eventually use the Infinity Gauntlet to restore everyone that Thanos snapped out of existence. Moments later, Hawkeye's cell phone rings and he hears the precious voice of his wife on the other end, kids playing in the background. Hawkeye got his family back. Similarly, in the last chapter of Job, God gave Job a double portion of all he'd lost, restored his marriage, gave him 10 more children (in addition to the 10 awaiting him in heaven) and allowed him to live happily to a ripe old age.

God's endgame includes a happy ending for everyone who loves him and is called according to his purpose. Troubles and tragedies are a part of life. But no matter what comes your way, you can carry on if you have *faith, friends*, and *foresight*.

CHAPTER TWO: THOR

In the previous chapter, we saw how Hawkeye dealt with the loss of his family. In this chapter, I'd like to zero in on another character from *Avengers: Endgame* who experiences a different kind of loss—Thor. While Thor certainly experienced his share of loss with the death of his father and brother in previous films, Thor's story arc in *Endgame* centers around his defeat at the hands of Thanos.

Generally acknowledged as the mightiest Avenger, Thor was the first to encounter the Mad Titan in the previous film, *Avengers: Infinity War*. In the opening scene of *Infinity War*, Thanos attacks Thor and his brother Loki in order to obtain one of the coveted Infinity Stones. Thor fights back, but for all his might, he falls before Thanos who stands over him gloating, "I know what it's like to lose. To feel so desperately that you're right, yet to fail nonetheless."

This failure haunts Thor throughout the movie. He convinces himself that the reason he couldn't defeat Thanos is that he didn't' have his fabled hammer Mjolnir. So, he sets off on a quest to forge a new hammer in the heart of a dying star. At the end of the movie, Thor arrives on earth with his new powerful hammer in hand, to confront Thanos before he can use the Infinity Stones to wipe out half of all life in the universe. Crackling with lighting, Thor launches himself toward Thanos and hurls the axe end of his new weapon right into Thanos' chest. Though mortally wounded, Thanos whispers to Thor, "You should have gone for the head," then snaps his fingers. Thor failed again. This time it cost billions of lives.

Thor's failure hangs over his head like a dark cloud throughout *Endgame*. Toward the beginning of the film, Tony Stark sees Thor sulking in a corner and asks, "What's wrong with him." Rocket Racoon aptly answers, "He thinks he failed. Which, of course, he did. But, you know, there's a lot of that going around, ain't there?"

Unable to overcome his sense of failure, Thor hermits himself away in a small Norwegian village where he wallows in self-pity, drinks himself into a stupor, plays video games all day, and packs on the pounds.

If anyone in Scripture could relate to Thor's struggle with failure, it's the Apostle Peter. Like Thor, Peter failed when it mattered most and his failure hung over his head like a dark cloud. Of course, Peter's not the only person to feel the sting of failure. We all do. Everybody fails at times. And sometimes those failures can feel overwhelming. Maybe you can relate to Thor or Peter. Perhaps you feel like a failure. Maybe you feel like throwing in the towel and just giving up.

Peter's story teaches us three things we need to know about failure if we hope to overcome it. First, we need to understand that failure is frequent.

FAILURE IS FREQUENT

Just as Thor failed multiple times to defeat Thanos, Peter frequently fails throughout Scripture.

You might recall the time Peter failed to walk on water. In Matthew 14, a thunderstorm threatens to sink Peter's small fishing boat when he suddenly spots Jesus walking on the water. Peter calls out, "Lord, if it's you, tell me to come to you on the water." So, Jesus beckoned Peter to come. Peter boldly climbs out of the boat and takes a few steps, momentarily mimicking his Savior. But when the wind and waves crash around him, Peter loses his faith and his footing. He plunges into the water and calls out for help. Jesus catches him, lifts him up, and says, "You have so little faith. Why did you doubt me?" (Matthew 14:31 NLT). Sopping wet and ashamed, Peter climbed back into the boat.

Of course, this wasn't Peter's first failure and it wouldn't be his last.

On the night before his crucifixion, Jesus prayed in the Garden of Gethsemane. He asked his three closest friends — Peter, James, and John — to stay awake and keep watch while he prayed. But when Jesus finished praying, he found all three disciples sleeping on the job. So, Jesus singles Peter out, saying, "Couldn't you watch with me even one hour? Keep watch and pray, so that you will not give in to temptation. For the spirit is willing, but the body is weak!" (Matthew 26:40-41 NLT). Peter failed, yet again.

Of course, his most devastating failure came the next morning. Earlier that night, Jesus predicted that Peter would deny knowing him three times. Peter adamantly responded, "Even if I have to die with you, I will never deny you!" (Matthew 26:35 NLT). Of course, Jesus was right and Peter was wrong. While Jesus stood trial, Peter waited in the courtyard. During the night, three different people accused Peter of being one of Jesus' followers and friends. Three times Peter vehemently denied it. As the guards led Jesus through the courtyard, his eyes met Peter's and Peter remembered what Jesus said. Suddenly Peter burst into tears and ran away. Peter failed Jesus when it mattered most.

Peter failed over and over in his life and his walk with Christ. But, as Rocket Racoon pointed out, "there's a lot of that going around, ain't there?" You've failed more times than you can remember. You fell down the first time you tried to walk. You almost drowned the first time you tried to swim, didn't you? Did you hit the ball the first time you swung a bat? Probably not. Failure is a part of life.

Thor finally figures that out when he's reunited with his mother on Asgard. He tells her about his battle with Thanos, concluding, "I was too late. I was just standing there. Some idiot with an axe." His mother replies, "Now, you're no idiot… A failure? Absolutely." But then she continues, "Do you know what that makes you? Just like everyone else… everyone fails."

Are you familiar with failure? Do you know the heartache of a failed marriage or a failed career? Do you feel like a failure as a father or a friend? Then welcome to humanity. Failure is a frequent part of life. But those failures don't have to characterize us or cripple us. Because not only is failure frequent, it's also forgivable.

FAILURE IS FORGIVABLE

Following his comforting conversation with his mother, Thor holds out his hand in anxious anticipation. You might recall that Thor's father, Odin, placed an enchantment on Thor's hammer Mjolnir, whispering the words, "Whosoever holds this hammer, if he be worthy, shall possess the power of Thor." Thanks to this magical spell no one can lift Mjolnir unless they are worthy of wielding it. When the mythic mallet flies into Thor's open hand, his eyes well up with tears as he realizes aloud, "I'm still worthy!" Despite his failure, he was still worthy.

Peter experienced a similar realization over breakfast one morning.

Following his failure, Peter appears ready to quit. Three years ago, Jesus called him away from his career as a fisherman to become a fisher of men. Yet, even after Jesus came back from the dead, Peter still felt like a failure. Rather than head toward Galilee like he was supposed to, Peter went back to what he knew best—fishing. He was ready to return to his old life and give up being a follower of Jesus. But you remember the story, don't you?

Peter and the others are out on the Sea of Galilee. They've been fishing all night with no success. Then Jesus shows up. He tells them to cast their nets one more time and they catch so many fish they can hardly haul in the net. This, by the way, is the very same miracle Jesus perform the first time he and Peter met (Luke 5). In the aftermath of this mighty miracle, Peter leaps into the water and swims ashore. Soon, Jesus and his disciples share a broiled breakfast on the beach. After the meal, Jesus asked Peter "Do you love me more than these?" (presumably pointing at the fish). Peter replies, "Yes, Lord, you know that I love you." Jesus responds, "Then take care of my sheep."

Two more times, Jesus asks, "Do you love me?" Two more times, Peter answers, "Yes, Lord." And two more times, Jesus commissions Peter, "Take care of my sheep." Since Peter denied Jesus three times, Jesus gave Peter three chances to affirm his love and loyalty.

Peter's failure wasn't unforgivable. In fact, Jesus ended their conversation with the very same words he used to commission Peter three years earlier: "Follow me" (Matthew 4:19, John 21:22). Peter was still worthy. Thanks to Jesus, Peter found forgiveness and a second chance.

And, praise God, the same can be true for you. Just as he did for Peter, Jesus offers to forgive all our flaws, faults, and failures. No matter how badly you've blown it, no matter how far you've fallen, forgiveness is available through Jesus Christ. The Bible assures us, "Through the blood of his Son, we are set free from our sins. God forgives our failures because of his overflowing kindness" (Ephesians 1:7 GWT). God forgives our failures. That's good news, isn't it?

So, first, we need to understand that failure is frequent—it's a part of life. Furthermore, we need to know that failure is forgivable—it doesn't disqualify us. And finally, we need to realize that failure is forgettable.

FAILURE IS FORGETTABLE

Dwelling on our defeats will only prevent future success. But by letting go of our failures, we can move forward toward victory. The Apostle Paul put it this way: "Forgetting what is behind and straining toward what is ahead, I press on toward the goal to win the prize for which God has called me heavenward in Christ Jesus" (Philippians 3:13-14 NLT). Paul refused to allow the failures of yesterday to prevent him from moving forward and accomplishing his goals.

The same could be said for Peter. He moved on. He pressed on. After Jesus recommissioned Peter on the beach that morning, Peter went on to become the most important and influential leader in church history. On the day of Pentecost, Peter preached to a standing-room-only crowd and led three thousand souls to Christ. He continued preaching Jesus in the synagogues and on the streets, performing mighty miracles to affirm his message. When religious rulers caught wind of Peter's preaching, they had him arrested. Peter stood before the very same High Council that condemned Jesus to death. Once again, some of them recognized Peter as one of Jesus' followers. But when they questioned Peter about Jesus, this time Peter didn't deny Christ. Instead, he announced, "Let me clearly state to all of you…There is salvation in no one else! God has given no other name under heaven by which we must be saved" (Acts 4:10-12 NLT). The Council demanded that Peter stop preaching about Jesus, but he replied, "We cannot stop telling about everything we have seen and heard" (Acts 4:20 NLT).

Despite their threats, with his life on the line, Peter didn't back down. He stood his ground and proudly proclaimed the name of Jesus. There in that courtroom, Peter got his second chance to stand up for Christ and he didn't fail. He continued spreading the Gospel all across the Roman world and led countless people to salvation through the name of Jesus. His failures became a distant memory—forgiven and forgotten.

Thor likewise got a second shot at success. In the climactic final battle of *Avengers: Endgame*, Thor and his fellow Avengers face off against Thanos one last time. As the battle begins, Thanos taunts them, "You could not live with your own failure. Where did that bring you? Back to me." But this time, Thanos fails. Together, Thor and the Avengers finally defeat Thanos and restore everyone that he snapped out of existence. In the end, having put his failures behind him, Thor sets off in search of new adventures. Perhaps it's time for you to do the same thing.

***

Maybe you've failed in school or your career. Maybe you've failed at relationships or in your Christian life. Maybe you've failed more times than you can count and you feel the weight of those failures every day. Don't give up! Don't let your failures define you or destroy you. Failure is a frequent part of life, but it's also forgivable and forgettable. Let's follow Peter's example. Let's embrace the forgiveness that Jesus offers. Let's forget what lies behind and press on toward the goal that God has set before us.

CHAPTER THREE: THE HULK

After designing and overseeing the construction of a gamma bomb, Dr. Bruce Banner organized the first test detonation in the New Mexico desert. But in an unforeseeable accident, Banner himself was caught in the blast and bombarded with gamma radiation. Afterward, Bruce found himself transformed, physically and psychologically, in times of anger and outrage into a seven-foot, one-thousand-pound beast of uncontrolled fury—the Incredible Hulk!

Throughout the previous Marvel movies, the brilliant and benign Dr. Banner dreads and despises the Hulk. He often refers to the Hulk as "the other guy," and desires nothing more than to find a cure for his unwanted transformations. Hulk and Banner are polar opposites. Banner is smart, while Hulk is stupid. Banner is puny, while Hulk is powerful. Banner is gentle, while Hulk is, in the words of Tony Stark, "a giant green rage monster."

In *Avengers: Endgame*, however, audiences met a completely unexpected version of the Hulk. After Tony Stark initially refuses to help the remaining Avengers achieve time travel, they turn to Bruce Banner, who has changed dramatically since we last saw him. The Avengers meet Bruce in a diner where they learn he's big and green all the time now, but with Bruce Banner's mind in control.

This version of Hulk, sometimes referred to as "Professor Hulk," was a pleasant surprise. Gone are the days of Bruce's anger control issues. He no longer wrestles with "the monster within." Instead, Bruce has learned to control, conquer, and channel his anger. No longer two separate personalities, this "Professor Hulk" is the best of both worlds—smart and strong.

In addition to being one of the most likable characters in the movie, Hulk also sets an excellent example for comic fans and Christ-followers alike. Throughout the three-hour film, Hulk demonstrates three qualities that every Christian ought to possess. First, the Hulk is persistent.

PERSISTENT

Hulk demonstrates impressive persistence in several ways.

In the diner where he meets his fellow Avengers, Hulk responds to Ant-Man's astonishment, saying, "I know. It's crazy. I'm wearing shirts now!" When asked how he accomplished his dramatic transformation, Hulk replies, "Five years ago we got our [butts] beat, except it was worse for me because I lost twice. First Hulk lost. Then Banner lost. Then we all lost…For years, I've been treating the Hulk like some kind of disease, something to get rid of. But then I start looking at him as the cure. Eighteen months in the gamma lab, I put the brains and the brawn together and now look at me. Best of both worlds." Despite past dead ends and disappointments, Bruce Banner never gave up. Once he recognized the potential of combining the best of attributes of Banner and Hulk, he sequestered himself in a laboratory, experimenting with gamma radiation until he found the solution he sought. He persisted.

Another example of Hulk's persistence is found in a deleted scene. When a downtown fire rages out of control, threatening the lives of several New Yorkers trapped in a skyscraper, Hulk leaps into action. Using a large satellite dish, Hulk scoops up the endangered citizens and bounds to safety. Gently lowering them to the street, Banner playfully announces, "Ding, ding! Ground floor. Everybody out." He even takes a moment to let the fire chief know the most effective way to quench the fire. This little scene reveals that Hulk hasn't given up on being a hero. He's still out on the streets doing what he can to help ordinary people.

Additionally, Hulk proves persistent when it comes to attaining time travel. When Tony refuses to help the team discover a way to travel back in time and recover the Infinity Stones, Bruce steps up. He works tirelessly to achieve the team's goal. Eventually, with Tony's help, Bruce's persistence pays off and the Avengers travel through time to set right what once went wrong.

Christians could benefit greatly from a Hulk-sized portion of persistence. The Bible says, "So let's not get tired of doing what is good. At just the right time we will reap a harvest of blessing if we don't give up" (Galatians 6:9 NLT). Similarly, Paul says, "I press on toward the goal to win the prize for which God has called me heavenward in Christ Jesus" (Philippians 3:14 NIV).

Spending your life in the service of God requires persistence and perseverance. It calls for determination and doggedness. You can't just give up when life gets hard, because it will get hard. There will always be another challenge to your faith, another obstacle to overcome, another Jericho in your path! It doesn't matter how many times you fall or get knocked down. What matters is how many times you get back up. So, follow Bruce Banner's example and be persistent.

Furthermore, the Hulk was positive.

POSITIVE

Another positive aspect of Hulk's character is his positivity. *Avengers: Endgame* not only shows "Professor Hulk" to be much more intelligent than the previous version, he's arguably one of the nicest people on the team!

In the diner scene, the Avengers' discussion gets interrupted when some kids approach their table, saying, "Excuse me, Mr. Hulk. Can we get a photo?" Hulk pleasantly replies, "One hundred percent, little person," then smiles for a selfie. He even encourages the kids to get a photo with Ant-Man, whom they don't recognize, because he doesn't want Ant-Man to feel left out.

Later, when Rocket Racoon and Nebula arrive at the Avengers' compound, the thrusters from their spaceship literally blow the contents of Ant-Man's tacos out of their shells. Nebula calls Ant-Man an idiot under her breath as she walks past. But as Hulk walks by, he smiles warmly and hands Ant-Man a couple of fresh tacos.

Afterward, Hulk travels to New Asgard to recruit Thor for the upcoming mission. When he senses Thor's fear and hesitation at the thought of confronting Thanos, Hulk offers some encouragement. "Now, I know that... guy... might scare you," he sympathizes. "I get it. You're in a rough spot, okay?

I've been there myself. And you want to know who helped me out of it? It was you. You helped me."

Smiling for selfies with kids, sharing his extra tacos with a teammate, and encouraging a discouraged, defeated friend are all ways Hulk radiates positivity. Once again, Christians would do well to follow his example.

The Bible commands, "So encourage each other and build each other up, just as you are already doing" (1 Thessalonians 5:11 NLT). Peter similarly instructs believers, saying, "Sympathize with each other. Love each other as brothers and sisters. Be tenderhearted, and keep a humble attitude." (1 Peter 3:8 NLT). In short, Christians are called to treat one another in a positive, encouraging way. Rather than tearing people down, we ought to look for ways to build them up. Treating others in a positive, uplifting way not only fulfills God's commands, but it also makes the world a better place. So, let's seek to have a Christ-like heart and a Hulk-like attitude.

Finally, in addition to being persistent and positive, the Hulk is purposeful.

PURPOSEFUL

During a pivotal scene, Hulk delivers one of the most profound and powerful lines of the movie. After successfully gathering all of the Infinity Stones and returning to their own time, a brief argument breaks out over who will wear the Infinity Gauntlet and undo the death and destruction wrought by Thanos. Thor insists on being the one, saying, "I'm the strongest Avenger, okay. So, this responsibility falls upon me." When Tony objects, Thor persists, "What do you think is coursing through my veins right now? Lightning!" That's when Hulk steps in, saying, "Lightning won't help you, pal. It's got to be me. You saw what those stones did to Thanos. They almost killed him. None of you could survive... The radiation is mostly gamma. It's like... I was made for this." In that moment, Hulk recognized a preordained, perhaps even divine, purpose to his life. He didn't always recognize his purpose, though.

Way back in the first Avengers movie, Tony and Bruce have a conversation about Bruce's hatred of the Hulk. Tony says, "Hey, I've read all about your accident. That much gamma exposure should have killed you." Bruce replies, "So you're saying that the Hulk... the other guy... saved my life? That's nice. It's a nice sentiment. Saved it for what?" Tony smirks and says, "I guess we'll find out." Seven years and several movies later, Bruce finally found out what he was saved to do. He discovered his purpose.

Have you discovered yours? Like Bruce Banner, you and I were created for a purpose and saved for a purpose. Pastor and author, Rick Warren, writes, "The purpose of your life is far greater than your own personal fulfillment, your peace of mind, or even your happiness. It's far greater than your family, your career, or even your dreams and ambitions. If you want to know why you were placed on this planet, you must begin with God. You were born by his purpose and for his purpose."

Scripture continually confirms this claim. God told the displaced people of Israel, "For I know the plans I have for you...plans to prosper you and not to harm you, plans to give you hope and a future" (Jeremiah 29:11 NIV). Likewise, the New Testament assures Christian, "And we know that God causes everything to work together for the good of those who love God and are called according to his purpose for them" (Romans 8:28 NLT). And, similarly, "For we are God's masterpiece. He has created us anew in Christ Jesus, so we can do the good things he planned for us long ago" (Ephesians 2:10 NLT).

God has a purpose and plan for each one of us. Like Bruce Banner, you may not be aware of your purpose at first. But, if you will seek God and search the Scriptures, then you'll discover God's purpose and plan for your life and you'll be able to join Hulk in saying, "I was made for this."

***

Ultimately, "Professor Hulk" seems like a significant improvement over his stupider, more savage incarnation. Not only is this version of Hulk charming and capable, but he also exemplifies the admirable attributes of persistence, positivity, and purposefulness. You and I would do well to follow in Hulk's gigantic footsteps.

Chapter Four:
Captain America

As mentioned in chapter two, Thor wields a special weapon—Mjolnir, an indestructible hammer that responds to his call and channels lightning. Thor's father, Odin, placed an enchantment on the hammer, saying, "Whosoever holds this hammer, if he be worthy, shall possess the power of Thor." Thanks to this magical spell no one can lift Mjolnir unless they are worthy of wielding it.

In fact, there's a scene in one of the previous Avengers films, *Age of Ultron*, where each of the Avengers takes turns trying to lift Thor's hammer. Hawkeye can't budge it and insists it's a trick of some kind. Bruce Banner tries and fails. Tony Stark puts on his Iron Man armor, but even jet propulsion doesn't give him enough thrust to move it. He claims it's rigged, that the hammer is somehow keyed to Thor's DNA or fingerprints. Thor replies, "That's a very, very interesting theory. I have a simpler one. You're all not worthy." One Avenger, however, brings Thor's theory into question. When Steve Rogers, better known as Captain America, wraps his hands around the hammer, Mjolnir shifts ever so slightly. Thor raises a surprised eyebrow, but then Steve lets go and humbly toss up his hands as if to say, "I give up. I can't lift it either." This scene subtlety foreshadows the most cheer-worthy moment in *Avengers: Endgame.*

In the climactic final battle between the Avengers and Thanos, Thor wields two weapons—Mjolnir and Storm Breaker (the new hammer he forged during *Infinity Wars*). But even armed with his powerful new weapon, Thor alone isn't a match for Thanos. That's when Captain America proves his worth. Just when it appears that Thanos will get the better of Thor, Mjolnir comes streaking through the air and crashes into Thanos. The hammer then returns to Captain America's outstretched hand. Cap wields the hammer in an unrelenting series of devastating blows against the Mad Titan and even calls down a barrage of lightning strikes.

Audiences erupted when they watched Captain America wielding Mjolnir. I literally pumped my fist and shouted when I first saw it. Of course, this scene raises questions about what it means to be worthy—an important question not only for Captain America, but also for Christians.

In the New Testament book of Philippians, the Apostle Paul writes this: "Just one thing: Live your life in a manner worthy of the gospel of Christ" (Philippians 1:27 HCSB). Other translations begin this verse "whatever happens" (NIV) or "above all else" (NLT). It seems of utmost importance that we live lives "worthy" of the Gospel. But how do we do that? What does it mean to be worthy?

Thankfully, Paul answers that question for us. In the following verses, he writes: "Then... I will know that you are standing together with one spirit and one purpose, fighting together for the faith, which is the Good News. Don't be intimidated in any way by your enemies. This will be a sign to them that they are going to be destroyed, but that you are going to be saved, even by God himself" (Philippians 1:27-28 NIV). In this brief passage, Paul describes four characteristics that define what it means to be worthy not only for Christians, but perhaps also for Captain America!

First, being worthy requires conviction!

CONVICTION

Paul tells the Philippian Christians that being worthy includes "standing strong with one purpose" (Philippians 1:27 NCV). Paul often urges his fellow believers to "be strong" or "stand firm" in the faith. In other words, you don't give up, you don't quit, you don't back down.

Captain America models this sort of conviction throughout *Avenger: Endgame*. Even after their devastating loss to Thanos, Steve never gives up. Before embarking on their mission to reclaim the Infinity Stones and undo the death and destruction Thanos wrought, Captain America reminds his fellow Avengers, "Five years ago, we lost. All of us. We lost friends. We lost family. We lost a part of ourselves. Today, we have a chance to take it all back... This is the fight of our lives. And we're going to win. Whatever it takes."

Those words—*whatever it takes*—become the Avengers' mantra. And during the final battle with Thanos, Captain America demonstrate that conviction. Beaten and bloody, Steve refused to stay down. Every time Thanos knocked him to the ground, he got back up. Outmatched and overpowered, Cap stood strong no matter what.

That's the kind of conviction God calls us to demonstrate when it comes to the Gospel—the truth of Jesus Christ.

Elsewhere, the Apostle Paul writes: "Our struggle is not against flesh and blood, but against the rulers, against the authorities, against the powers of this dark world and against the spiritual forces of evil in the heavenly realms. Therefore put on the full armor of God, so that when the day of evil comes, you may be able to stand your ground, and after you have done everything, to stand. Stand firm!" (Ephesians 6:12-14 NIV).

The devil, demons, and this dark world are going to knock us down and beat us up. Our determination to live our lives for Christ is bound to be tested in ways we've never imagined. But no matter what trials or temptations we face, we need to stand strong. Whatever challenges you face, whatever battle you're fighting, God will give you the victory as long as you stand strong in him. Whatever it takes.

First, living lives worthy of the Gospel requires conviction. Further, being worthy requires cooperation.

COOPERATION

As Paul continues, he explains that being worthy means "standing together with one spirit and one purpose, fighting together for the faith" (Philippians 1:27 NLT). Other translations say, "stand united" (MSG) or "work together as one" (NCV). God doesn't just call us to believe; he calls us to belong. That means we're all part of a team. We stand *together*. We fight the good fight *together*.

Part of what makes Captain America worthy is his ability to lead, inspire, and fight alongside a team. Toward the beginning of *Endgame*, Tony Stark—Iron Man—recalls a conversation he had with Steve in a previous film—*Avengers: Age of Ultron.*

During a disagreement, Tony argues, "A hostile alien army came charging through a hole in space… How were you guys planning on beating that?" Steve responds with one word: "Together." Tony pessimistically replies, "We'll lose." Steve answers, "Then we'll do that together, too." Steve understood the value of teamwork.

In the climactic final fight, Captain America rallies every hero in Marvel's Cinematic Universe with the familiar battle cry, "Avengers Assemble!"

To assemble means to come together. That's what we're called to do as followers of Christ. In fact, that's what we're called. Period. The Greek word translated *church* in the Bible is *ecclesia.* The most literal definition of that word is simply *an assembly.* That's what the church is—God's people assembled.

The Philippian church, to whom Paul wrote, was a hodgepodge of believers from a variety of backgrounds, with different personalities, and sometimes conflicting opinions, yet they found a way to work together. They understood that they were stronger together. And because they did, lives were changed—people were saved.

And as we follow their example, the same will happen.

Whether you want to help feed the hungry, or house orphans, or provide school supplies or Christmas presents for local children, or share the gospel—none of us can do alone what all of us can do together. We can accomplish more and have a greater impact on our communities and our country when we work together.

If we want to live lives worthy of the Gospel of Jesus Christ, we need to cooperate with one another, stand united, and work together as one. Furthermore, Paul tells us that living lives worthy of the Gospel requires contending.

CONTENDING

Again, Paul says that being worthy means "fighting together for the faith" (Philippians 1:27 NLT). Another translation says, "striving side by side [as if in combat] for the faith of the gospel" (Philippians 1:27 AMP). We have to fight—to contend—for the faith.

Before becoming the super-solider, Captain America, Steve Rogers was just a skinny kid from Brooklyn. During WWII, Steve tried again and again to enlist but he was always rejected because of his long list of health issues. He was too sickly to serve. After yet another failed attempt to enlist, his buddy, Bucky Barnes, confronts him, asking, "Why are you so keen to fight?" Steve answers, "Bucky, come on! There are men laying down their lives. I got no right to do any less than them." Both before and after becoming Captain America, Steve was eager to fight because he knew what he was fighting for and what he was fighting against.

So, what are we fighting for?

Like Paul, Jude writes, "I felt compelled to write and urge you to contend for the faith that was once for all entrusted to God's holy people" (Jude 3 NIV). Contend for the faith. Fight for the faith. What does that mean?

As we already read in Ephesians 6, our battle is not against flesh and blood. Rather, the Christian life is a never-ending struggle against evil, both within ourselves and in the world.

We don't fight an earthly enemy, but a spiritual battle against sin and Satan. Paul describes our battle, saying:

"We are human, but we don't wage war as humans do. We use God's mighty weapons, not worldly weapons, to knock down the strongholds of human reasoning and to destroy false arguments. We destroy every proud obstacle that keeps people from knowing God. We capture their rebellious thoughts and teach them to obey Christ." (2 Corinthians 10:3-5 NLT)

We are called to defend our faith with reason and truth. We stand opposed to false religions and worldviews that are hostile toward God. We do this by spreading the Gospel—the Good News of Jesus Christ. God counts on us to "take captives," which means surrendering our own thoughts and beliefs to Christ, but also leading others to do the same. Our goal is not to destroy our enemies; but rather, to make them our allies. The Gospel—the truth about Jesus Christ—is the power of God to save everyone who believes.

So, according to Paul, being worthy requires conviction, cooperation, contending, and—finally—courage.

COURAGE

Paul urges the Philippian Christians to fight the good fight "without being frightened in any way by those who oppose you" (Philippians 1:28 NIV). Another translation says, "Don't be intimidated in any way by your enemies" (NLT).

Courage is essential to living lives worthy of the Gospel.

Courage is also one of Captain America's strengths. Another scene from *Captain America: The First Avenger* takes place before Steve Rogers received the super-soldier serum that transforms him into Captain America. Despite Steve's physical frailties,

Dr. Abraham Erskine sees something of value in him and enrolls him in Project: Rebirth. But the man in charge, Colonel Chester Philips, is unimpressed.

"You put a needle in that kid's arm it's gonna go right through him," Colonel Philips complains. Watching Steve's feeble attempt to do jumping jacks, he adds, "Look at that. He's makin' me cry." Erskine replies, "I am looking for qualities beyond the physical." Finally, to prove his point, Col. Philips grabs a grenade, pulls the pin, then says, "You don't win wars with niceness, doctor. You win wars with guts," as he tosses the grenade toward the recruits. While the rest of his fellow soldiers duck and run for cover, Steve throws himself on top of the grenade and shouts, "Get away! Get Back!" Moments later, he realizes that he threw himself onto a dummy grenade.

That's courage.

In *Captain America* #444, another mythical member of the Avengers, Hercules, explains to Steve, "On Olympus, we measure Wisdom against Athena... Speed against Hermes... Power against Zeus. But we measure Courage... against Captain America."

The thing is—courage isn't just for superheroes or soldiers.

We tend to equate courage with heroism—firefighters running into a burning building, police arresting an armed criminal, or perhaps even early Christians facing violent persecution. We think of courage as something extraordinary, something unusual, or something people are called upon to exhibit only in dangerous, life-threatening situations. But most of the time, we don't think we need it.

We just don't see "courage" as an everyday necessity. But that's a mistake. Courage is not just for extreme situations.

Courage is basic to the exercise of every other virtue. Courage is required of God's people every day. It takes courage to do the right thing in a difficult situation. It takes courage to own up to your mistakes and confess your faults. It takes courage to give generously in a floundering economy or to ask for help when you need it. It takes courage to stand up and speak up for Christ.

Courage is foundational to virtually every virtue. So much so, that it's impossible to mature in Christ without it. It's impossible to consistently live lives worthy of the Gospel as long as we're dominated by fear instead of courage. Without courage, all of our other virtues will be weak and easily compromised. They'll fade away at the slightest challenge.

When Joshua took over as leader of the Israelites, God told him, "This is my command—be strong and courageous! Do not be afraid or discouraged" (Joshua 1:9 NLT). God actually repeats that command fourteen times in the Bible. God's command to Joshua is his command to you—*be strong and courageous*.

***

So, what does it mean to be *worthy*? To live lives *worthy* of the Gospel? Being worthy requires *conviction*—standing strong with one purpose, *cooperation*—working together as one, *contending*—fighting the good fight of faith, and *courage*—without being frightened in any way.

Captain America has long been my favorite Avenger because he embodies these Christian virtues. These characteristics are what made Cap worthy of wielding Thor's mythical hammer, Mjolnir. And these characteristics are what make our lives worthy of the Gospel of Jesus Christ.

CHAPTER FIVE:
BLACK WIDOW & IRON MAN

As we bring this study to a close, I would be remiss if I didn't include the two Avengers who made the ultimate sacrifice. In two of the most dramatic moments of the movie, Black Widow and Iron Man each sacrifice their lives to save the universe and defeat the treacherous titan, Thanos. The deaths of these beloved comic-book characters spurred strong emotional responses from fans, many of them wiping tears from their cheeks in the theaters. What movie-goers might have missed, however, are the powerful parallels between the death of these characters and the death of Jesus Christ. Whether or not these parallels were intentional, these cinematic sacrifices take on greater significance when viewed through a Christian lens.

Much like Black Widow and Iron Man, Jesus sacrificed his own life to save the world. And I'd like to point out three provocative parallels between the death of these superheroes and the death of our Savior. Let's jump right in.

First, these heroic deaths were all voluntary.

VOLUNTARY

Have you ever volunteered to do something? Perhaps as a kid, you volunteered to help Mom with the housekeeping or to shovel the driveway in the winter. Maybe you volunteer for community programs, at school, or here at church. There is a big difference between volunteering yourself to do something—willingly giving yourself for some cause—and doing something only out of obligation or because someone forced you to do it, isn't there?

Part of what made the deaths of Black Widow and Iron Man so moving and emotional for audiences is that neither of them was killed by an enemy; rather, they both laid down their lives willingly—voluntarily. This is especially true of Black Widow. While on their quest to acquire the Soul Stone—one of the six Infinity Stones—Black Widow and Hawkeye travel to a desolate world called Vormir, where they face a seemingly impossible decision.

The keeper of the stone, Red Skull, tells them, "In order to take the stone, you must lose that which you love. An everlasting exchange. A soul for a soul." One of them must sacrifice their life in order to claim the Soul Stone. Knowing what's at stake and how many people are counting on them, both Hawkeye and Black Widow are willing to give their lives. So much so, that they begin fighting for the opportunity to sacrifice themselves. In the end, Black Widow wins and leaps from the craggy cliffs to her death. Her life, however, wasn't taken from her; it was freely given.

The same is true of Jesus Christ.

Before ever arriving at the cross, Jesus once said, "The Father loves me because I sacrifice my life so I may take it back again. No one can take my life from me. I sacrifice it voluntarily. For I have the authority to lay it down when I want to and also to take it up again" (John 10:17-18 NLT).

When we reflect on the brutality and bloodshed Jesus experienced on the cross, we might wonder—couldn't Jesus have stopped it? Couldn't he have fought back? Jesus is the all-powerful Son of God. When the soldier raised the mallet to drive the nails, surely with the flex of his biceps, with a clench of the fist, Jesus could have resisted. As the old hymn says, "He could have called ten thousand angels to destroy the world and set him free." But he didn't. He chose to sacrifice himself.

The Romans who nailed Jesus to the cross didn't take his life; he gave it. Had the soldier hesitated, Jesus would have swung the hammer himself. He knew how; he was no stranger to driving nails. As a carpenter, he knew what it took. As a Savior, he knew what it meant. And as the hand of Jesus opened for the spike, the doors of heaven opened for you.

So, first, these valiant deaths were voluntary. Furthermore, all these deaths were vicarious.

VICARIOUS

Vicarious means taking the place of another person or serving as a substitute. Both Iron Man and Black Widow died vicarious death because they both died so that others could live. This is, again, especially evident in Black Widow's death.

In the scene mentioned earlier, Black Widow pleads with Hawkeye to let her be the one to die, saying, "I'm trying to save your life, you idiot." But Clint responds, "Yeah, well, I don't want you to, how's that? Natasha, you know what I've done. You know what I've become." If you'll recall, Clint lost his family at the beginning of the film. He didn't take that loss well. He becomes a bitter, grief-driven vigilante, violently wreaking bloody revenge on any bad guys he can catch.

Nevertheless, Natasha graciously replies, "Well, I don't judge people on their worst mistakes."

To be honest, this scene didn't sit well with me. I walked out of the theater thinking, "It should have been Hawkeye. He went down a dark path. He murdered people. That's not okay. This was his chance to redeem himself. Instead, he gets to go home to his wife and kids and live happily ever after, while Natasha dies in his place." It wasn't until I watched it a second time that it hit me: Isn't that exactly what Jesus did for me?

Hawkeye deserved to die. He didn't deserve to be forgiven and live happily ever after. But Natasha loved Clint. Even knowing what he had become, she withheld judgment. She showed mercy and grace, and then gave her life in his place. This is the Gospel in a nutshell.

Maybe you haven't gone on a violent killing streak, but you and I have sinned against God in so many ways. We deserve to be punished for our sins. We don't deserve to live happily ever after in Heaven. Yet, Jesus came to earth full of grace and mercy and then gave his life in my place. We call it substitutionary atonement.

The Bible says, "When we were utterly helpless, Christ came at just the right time and died for us sinners. Now, most people would not be willing to die for an upright person, though someone might perhaps be willing to die for a person who is especially good. But God showed his great love for us by sending Christ to die for us while we were still sinners." (Romans 5:6-8 NLT).

My mistake was thinking that Hawkeye could redeem himself. He couldn't. Neither can we. But just as Natasha gave her life to give Clint a second chance, Jesus gave his life to redeem you and me. I can just imagine Jesus shouting, "I'm trying to save your life, you idiot!"

Of course, Hawkeye wasn't the only person Natasha saved. Earlier in the scene, Black Widow reminds Hawkeye, "If we don't get that stone, billions of people stay dead." Because Natasha sacrificed her life to retrieve the Soul Stone, the Avengers were able to use the Infinity Gauntlet to restore everyone that Thanos snapped out of existence. She died so that billions of people could be raised from the dead. That's just what Jesus did. Jesus literally gave his life so that billions of people would be raised from the dead and live again. He died so that we could live.

So, the deaths of these Avengers point us to Jesus in that they were voluntary deaths, vicarious deaths, and—finally—they were also victorious deaths.

VICTORIOUS

For centuries—millennia, perhaps—Thanos led his armies across the galaxy, conquering worlds and killing half their inhabitants. While Black Widow's sacrifice made it possible for the Avengers to restore everyone Thanos previously killed, Thanos himself remained a threat. If he could get his hands on the Infinity Stones, he could just do it all again. The final victory came only when Iron Man sacrificed his life.

In the climactic final battle, Iron Man manages to pry the Infinity Stones loose from Thanos' clutches and incorporates them into his own nano-tech gauntlet. Accessing the combined power of the stones, Iron Man snaps his fingers and turns Thanos and his invasion forces to ash. The incredible power surge caused by the stones, however, proves too much for

Tony's frail human body. Iron Man sacrifices his own life to defeat Thanos and gain the victory.

Incidentally, the name Thanos comes from the Greek word for *death* (*thanatos*). It seems Marvel's Avengers and humanity, in general, share a common enemy. The Bible tells us, "Sin came into the world because of what one man did, and with sin came death. This is why everyone must die—because everyone sinned" (Romans 5:12 NCV).

Ever since the Garden of Eden, death has been the archenemy of humanity—and death always wins. The odds that you will eventually die in a car crash are 1:125. The chance of you dying in a fire is 1:4,000,000. The odds of you being killed by a purple-tinged titan from another planet are probably nil. But, the odds of you dying are 1:1. To paraphrase Thanos, death is *inevitable*. It comes to every living thing. For millennia, death has stalked its prey with exacting precision—a 100% success rate. That is, until Jesus.

Unlike Iron Man, when Jesus died to save the universe, he didn't stay dead. Jesus triumphantly conquered death when he got up and walked out of his grave and, in so doing, he opened the path to eternal life—life without death.

Looking forward to the Second Coming of Christ, the Apostle Paul writes:

> *It will happen in a moment, in the blink of an eye, when the last trumpet is blown. For when the trumpet sounds, those who have died will be raised to live forever. And we who are living will also be transformed. For our dying bodies must be transformed into bodies that will never die; our mortal bodies must be transformed into immortal bodies. Then… this Scripture will be fulfilled: "Death*

is swallowed up in victory. O death, where is your victory? O death, where is your sting?" For sin is the sting that results in death… But thank God! He gives us victory over sin and death through our Lord Jesus Christ. (1 Corinthians 15:52-57 NLT)

Jesus defeated death (literally *Thanos*) so that we could live forever with him in victory. Eternal life is a free gift to those who put their faith in Jesus. He died for us. Let's live for him.

***

These are three poignant parallels between the deaths of these Marvel superheroes and the death of our Mighty Savior. Their deaths were *voluntary*—their lives given, not taken. Their deaths were *vicarious*—they died so that others could live. Their deaths were *victorious*—they defeated the enemy and won the victory.

If you haven't put your faith in Jesus and accepted him as your Savior, just know that Jesus is Earth's mightiest hero. He wants to be your hero, too! He gave his life to save yours and invites you to enjoy eternal life with him.

CONCLUSION

While the characters showcased in *Avengers: Endgame* are all flawed fictional heroes, many of their actions and attitudes point beyond themselves to a hero that's both real and super—Jesus Christ.

Perhaps one of the reasons audiences flocked to see *Avengers: Endgame* is that people possess a deep inner longing for a hero. I believe this spiritual hunger for heroes is woven into the fabric of the human heart. God built us with a persistent longing for a rescuer who would bring help when we don't see help coming. We dream of a hero to step up and save the day.

Fittingly, the Bible says, "the Lord is an avenger" (1 Thessalonians 4:6 HCSB). Jesus is the hero we've all been searching for—the first and mightiest Avenger! Everything the Avengers aspire to be in comics, cartoons, and cinema, Jesus is in reality... and so much more. He is truly earth's mightiest hero, and he stands ready to be your hero if you'll let him.

Incidentally, the Bible reveals God's endgame, saying, "God sent his Son into the world not to judge the world, but to save the world through him" (John 3:17 NLT). God's endgame is "to save the world" through Jesus, and that includes you. Put your faith in him, and you'll discover that Jesus is the greatest superhero of them all!

ABOUT THE AUTHOR

MILD-MANNERED MINISTER BY DAY, SCOTT OFTEN SPENDS HIS WEEKENDS IN A CAPE AND COWL! HE IS CO-FOUNDER OF COSTUMERS FOR CHRIST, A NON-PROFIT MINISTRY THAT USES COMICS AND COSPLAY TO SHARE THE STORY OF CHRIST. HE'S THE AWARD-WINNING AUTHOR OF *HOLY HEROES: THE GOSPEL ACCORDING TO DC & MARVEL* AND *THE HOLY HEROES DEVOTIONAL*, AND ILLUSTRATOR OF *JESUS CHRIST: THE WORLD'S GREATEST HERO!* SCOTT LIVES WITH HIS FAMILY IN PALMYRA, ILLINOIS, WHERE HE PASTORS BLOOMING GROVE CHRISTIAN CHURCH.

WWW.HOLYHEROES.ORG

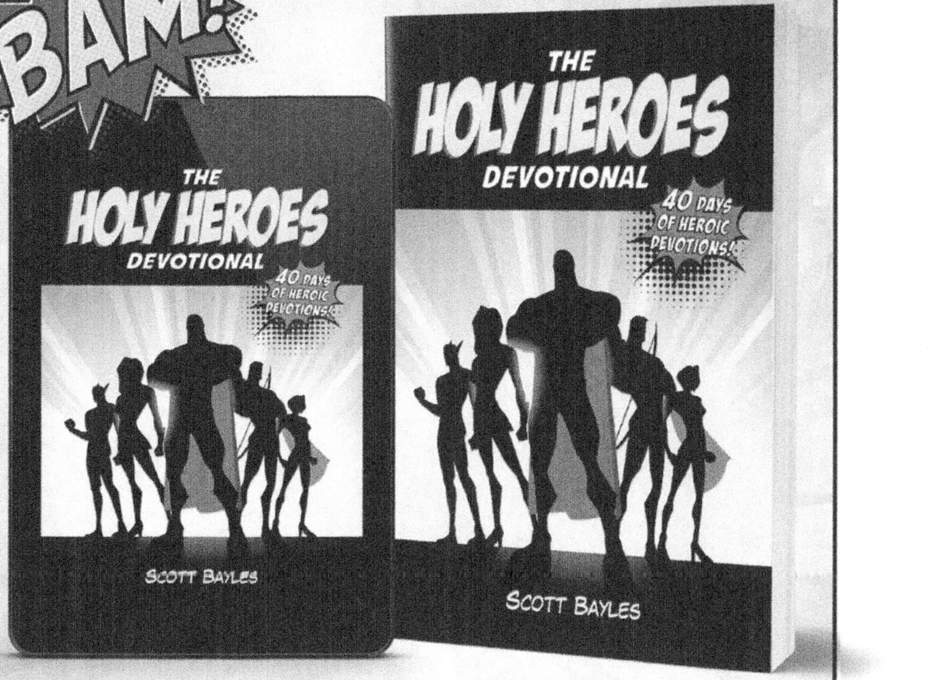

Made in United States
North Haven, CT
04 October 2025

80390130R00036